THE
ORVIS®
BOOK OF DOGS

Photography
Denver Bryan

Text
Tom Davis

Foreword
Paul Fersen

THE LYONS PRESS
GUILFORD, CONNECTICUT
AN IMPRINT OF THE GLOBE PEQUOT PRESS

Orvis is a registered trademark of The Orvis Company, Manchester, Vermont.
Visit Orvis at www.orvis.com.

The Lyons Press is an imprint of The Globe Pequot Press.

10 9 8 7 6 5 4 3 2 1

Printed in China
Designed by Nancy Freeborn

The Steve Smith quote on page 5 is from the book *Just Labs.*

The John Sergeant Wise quote on page 26 is from his 1897 book *Diomed: The Life, Travels,
and Observations of a Dog.*

ISBN 978-1-59921-030-8

Library of Congress Cataloging-in-Publication Data is available on file.

To buy books in quantity for corporate use
or incentives, call **(800) 962–0973**
or e-mail **premiums@GlobePequot.com.**

For Tanner, Tule, Trouble, Taylor—four dogs that I have so far owned and loved in my life. Each has left me with countless hours of wonderful companionship both afield and at home.

—Denver Bryan

To the gang from Andy's Acres—Bwana, Donny, John, Roscoe, and The Skipper—and to the dogs who show us the way: Belle, Bishop, Butch, Chase, Ernie, Ilsa, Pip, Sadie, and Sidney.

—Tom Davis

Contents

Foreword

There is a common perception among people that dogs are the descendants of wolves, domesticated by early man. It's as if somehow a half-wild man some twenty thousand years ago, who spent every waking moment simply trying to subsist, had the time and intelligence to take another wild creature and, by selective breeding, breed the wildness out of perhaps the wildest of creatures. It's a wonderfully romantic premise.

Recently a more plausible theory has been put forth: the wolf, in fact, domesticated himself and became the dog. The theory is that as man evolved from a nomad to a villager, he created permanent areas near the village where food waste, bones, and whatever else he discarded made for easy foraging. Those wolves that had the least fear of man and fled the shortest distances began to breed. Evolution accelerated because of circumstance. Cooperative pack behavior became unnecessary, and proximity to man became necessary. The wolf became the dog, and perhaps the most mutually beneficial relationship on earth came to be. For anthropologists and biologists, this is magnificent grist on which to chew, but for those of us who simply love the dog, we care only that it happened.

Though it is probable that early man used his dog for labor and protection, it is most certain that he used his dog to help him find food; success or failure in that quest was a simple matter of life or death. The factor of life or death long ago slipped the lead, and sustenance is a foregone conclusion, but the desire in some men and dogs to hunt has withstood the evolution of convenience. It is as strong now in those of us who carry fine guns as it was in the first man to carry a spear with a dog by his side. At Orvis we love dogs, but we particularly love the dogs that stay closest to their original mission as partners with man in his quest for game and sustenance.

From the first time a hunter sees the litter and his eyes fall on that one puppy whose precocious antics portend magnificent feats afield, to the day a saddened partner lays his trusted friend in the ground wrapped in a tattered blanket, there are myriad moments of such unfettered cooperation as to defy anything that man can conjure. A dog may have faults, but they are not the vices of disloyalty, dishonesty, and pretentiousness. Only man bears these. Those of us who hunt with dogs have the privilege of working in tandem with a partner whose only desire is to do that for which he was bred and trained and whose greatest reward is the simple acknowledgment of a hand on the head or a scratch behind the ears.

In a world that has become far too mean and whose values have eroded, in a world where selflessness is often replaced by selfishness, there is one last bastion of pure honesty between two creatures that have trod this earth together for thousands of years. Only in the field, looking in the eyes of a great hunting dog, can a hunter find true honesty, courage, and trust.

Whether in fact the wolf domesticated himself and became the dog or man managed to have sense enough to domesticate the wolf is not important. In either case the purest relationship man enjoys is the result. This book is about that relationship. Denver Bryan's magnificent photographs freeze those moments when everything we admire is so apparent. Tom Davis's text, layered with quote and anecdote, lays bare the pure emotion we feel when dogs do what dogs were truly meant to do. In the Orvis culture, perhaps nothing engenders unabashed admiration quite like a great hunting dog. This book explains why.

PAUL FERSEN
Outdoor Retail Merchandise Manager
The Orvis Company

At Home

::

FAMILY DOG

Like most Labs these days, Maggie was a full-time family dog—to use the term that seems to have replaced the suddenly unfashionable pet. There's a reason, after all, that the Lab is far-and-away the most popular breed in America. There are a host of reasons, actually, but the point is that flushing and/or retrieving gamebirds has become for many Labs a sideline to their primary roles as playmates, family companions, and in-house therapy dogs, their contagious enthusiasm and affectionate, ebullient personalities helping keep everybody on an even emotional keel as they negotiate the tricky currents of life in the twenty-first century.

Golden retriever.

Happily for Maggie, the head of her household in southeastern Wisconsin, a dentist named Michael Markgraf, was a duck hunter. So for a few days every fall she was able to fulfill the role that has defined the Labrador breed and shaped its development for the last two hundred years—if not longer, if you count the time the Lab's direct progenitor, the St. John's dog of Newfoundland, was used to retrieve fish—cod, for example—that had thrashed free of their hooks. And as the writer Jim Harrison (an owner of Labs and English setters) has observed: a dog is always happiest when it's doing the job it was bred to do.

Having taken a day off from work so he could avoid the weekend crowds, Markgraf rose in the wee hours of the morning, bundled Maggie into his truck, and headed for Lake Puckaway—a sprawling, reed-stippled body of water in the central part of the state and a choice spot for late-season waterfowling.

> A dog is always happiest when it's doing the job it was bred to do.

The boat landing was deserted, just as Markgraf had hoped, and the weather—stinging snow squalls propelled by a gusty north wind—was a duck hunter's dream. There was a marshy point about a mile from the landing that Markgraf figured would be the ideal place to set up his decoy spread; with the boat tucked back in the cattails he and Maggie would be in perfect position when the big, red-legged mallards, fresh from the prairies of Canada, came pouring in. On a day like this, it was only a matter of time.

Navigating by compass in the predawn gloom, Markgraf aimed his

Springer spaniel.

fourteen-foot duck boat for the point. He knew he should have replaced the

battered craft long ago, but it was a vessel that held a lot of sentimental

value—it had been his father's—and duck hunters, as much if not more than any other class of sportsmen, are apt to be swayed by sentiment, by the pull of time-honored traditions. Maybe he'd start shopping for a new boat come spring.

The ride was rough. Maggie scrabbled for purchase, her nails scratching the hull as she struggled to stay upright. But the old boat seemed able to handle the heavy seas, its bow plowing stubbornly through the swells. Markgraf was so intent on maintaining his compass heading that it took a while for him to realize that something wasn't right, that the boat was canted at a strange angle. He looked around and saw, to his horror, that the stern was almost completely awash. The gas tank was floating; the decoys bobbed on their anchor lines.

Instinctively, Markgraf swung the tiller and turned the boat toward shore. He knew he was in a dangerous situation: exactly a year earlier, on this same lake and under remarkably similar conditions, a duck boat had capsized. The dogs made it safely to shore. The hunters didn't.

Thinking of nothing but keeping the motor running, Markgraf managed to get about three-quarters of the way back before the outboard sputtered and stopped. Then, in a heartbeat, he found himself up to his neck in the icy water, desperately clinging to the overturned hull. He wasn't wearing a life jacket, and the boat had capsized so quickly that he hadn't had time to grab the flotation cushion he'd been sitting on.

Maggie was in the water, too, and as she swam in circles around the boat Markgraf tried to get her to swim to shore—where presumably she'd be able to summon help—by hollering "Maggie, go!" But the sturdy yellow Lab would just paddle a few yards, glance over her shoulder as if to say 'Aren't you coming, too?' and turn back.

GOING BEYOND LUCK

Realizing that he'd die of exposure if he stayed with the boat, Markgraf tried to backstroke to shore. But it was no use: he kept getting turned around, and he was losing strength rapidly. His hands and feet were growing numb and becoming as heavy and unresponsive as if they were blocks of petrified wood. He was on the verge of giving up—but then he looked at Maggie. Their gazes met, and her soulful eyes told him she knew what was at stake. Normally Maggie couldn't stand to have her tail touched. But when Markgraf grasped it, she understood perfectly.

> "No water too big or cold or deep, no distance too far. For hunting Labs, there is only wave and wind and sky, and the shout of strong-hearted ancestors in their ears, urging them on."
>
> —Steve Smith

"There was a lot of nonverbal communication between us," Markgraf recalled. "How do you explain to a dog, 'I'll grab your tail, and you'll tow me to shore?' All I said was 'Maggie, go!'"

It seemed as if it took Maggie an eternity to swim those 250 yards—but when existence itself hangs in the balance, seconds feel like minutes, and minutes feel like hours. It was all Markgraf could do to simply hang on and keep

ACTION: THE WORK OF A RETRIEVER

The enthusiasm and *joie de vivre* of a retriever doing what it loves to do are infectious—if not downright addictive. There's no doubt that thousands of men and women are hooked on it. Oh, they maintain a façade of normalcy—putting in their time at work and going through the motions of being productive members of society—but their every waking moment is consumed by thoughts of their retrievers, of when they'll have their next opportunity to hang a whistle around their neck, grab a bag of dummies, and go training. Like their dogs, they just can't get enough.

There's a sense in which the desire to retrieve is indiscriminate. From the perspective of a dog that comes from a long line of fetchers, it's not so much *what* they retrieve, but *that* they retrieve. You have to take the bitter with the sweet, though, such as when your dog trots up to you bearing something old, rotten, and very, very ripe with a proud expression that seems to say, "Hey, check out this dead carp I found. Isn't it cool?" Still, these are *hunting* dogs—and adding the scent of a gamebird to the retrieving party is pretty much like throwing gasoline on a fire.

breathing. Then, miraculously, his leaden feet scraped against something solid. They'd made it!

While Markgraf slogged the last few yards to shore (he may have kissed the ground when he got there, but that's just speculation), Maggie rolled on her back in the sand, kicking her legs in the air as if the entire ordeal had been more fun than chasing a tomcat up a tree.

Later that same morning, after standing in the shower until the hot water ran out and unwittingly scalding his frozen feet in the process, Markgraf returned to Lake Puckaway. He recovered his boat, motor, oars, decoys,

> Retrieving has become for many Labs a sideline to their primary roles as playmates, family companions, and in-house therapy dogs.

Brittany

An industrious hunter with a bouncy, quick-striding gait, the Brittany, named for the region in northwestern France where it originated, is one of the few sporting breeds developed not by landed aristocrats, but by people of common means. Historically, in fact, its small size and tailless, somewhat unprepossessing appearance endeared it to poachers, who found that it aroused less suspicion than other dogs. Versatile and companionable, the Brittany is a terrific choice for the sportsman who wants a pointing dog that's also a natural retriever and does a creditable job with a minimum of training.

One piece of gun dog terminology that frequently confuses the uninitiated is non-slip retriever. The term conjures up all sorts of bizarre images, but what it refers to is a dog that remains at its handler's side—not "slipped," that is (meaning "unleashed")—until directed to retrieve. A non-slip retriever, then, is expected to remain perfectly obedient—even when faced with the sorest temptations. This exuberant golden must have skipped class that day.

The retrieving breeds seem to have a natural affinity for water and will seize any opportunity to swim, splash, or simply frolic in it. Trouble is, while they eventually leave the water, not all the water leaves them. This raises one of life's great unanswered questions: Why do dogs invariably shake on you?

and even the cushion he hadn't been able to get his hands on when he capsized. The only things he lost were his shotgun and shell box.

"It was eerie," said Markgraf of returning to the place where, only hours earlier, his life had nearly been snatched away. "There was nobody out there. All I could think was that it was a good thing Maggie didn't go to shore without me. I'd say I was damn lucky—but this went beyond luck."

For the record, about a week later Markgraf and Maggie climbed back in the saddle and went duck hunting again—in a brand new boat. For the Lab, it was business as usual. Her owner, on the other hand, admitted to being "nervous as hell."

YOU BET YOUR LIFE

Now, stories of dogs performing heroic deeds—putting themselves in harm's way, risking their own lives to save their masters' lives— are nothing new. The lore and literature of dogdom are replete with examples, and while a certain percentage of these tales are undoubtedly apocryphal they still serve to illustrate some abiding and fundamental truths about the canine character. Or at least its nobler aspects, dogs being no less various in terms of their character than people are—although the sporting breeds are obviously the cream of the crop.

The question Maggie's story begs is, Would she have responded the same way if she and Markgraf weren't "family"? In other words, if Maggie had been an outside dog—housed in a kennel instead of ensconced in the home, her contact with the family limited, and her role largely restricted to that of occasional hunting companion—would the bond then between dog and man have been powerful enough to generate the crucial nonverbal communication Markgraf spoke of? Would Maggie have even stuck around, circling the capsized boat while she waited for her master to figure out their next

Stories of dogs performing heroic deeds are nothing new.

move? Or would she have simply lit out for shore? Would she have allowed her tail—her don't-touch-there place—to be used as a tow-rope?

Clearly, the answer is impossible to know with absolute certainty. But you can be damn sure that Michael Markgraf is glad he didn't have to bet his life on it.

HOUSE DOGS AND KENNEL DOGS

For decades, if not centuries, the conventional wisdom was that hunting dogs should not live in the house—with their master and his family, that is—except under special circumstances. A dog recovering from illness or injury, for example, might earn a temporary exemption; ditto a female that was about to whelp or was nursing a litter of pups.

The reasoning behind this prohibition was a bit vague, but the thrust of it was that dogs allowed to live in the house got "soft." Their ability to cope with cold weather, icy water, and the rigors of the hunt in general was compromised; the sharp, bright edge of their instincts became dull and blunted.

Puppies For Sale
Father-- Rawhides Clown
Mother - No River's Hannah
(PJ Wildfire Grand Daughter)
Tim Brewster
Must Sell !!

A little knowledge is a dangerous thing. Because dogs so clearly love to run, play, and simply explore their world a lot of people assume that being confined must be torture to them. Nonsense: dogs take to crates, kennels, and "boxes" readily, especially if they're introduced to them as pups (German short-hair pointer puppies).

They view them as places of security and safety—querencias, if you will—and as long as they're given plenty of attention and exercise, kenneled dogs are typically as happy as clams (pointer puppies).

During hunting trips, field trials, or extended training sessions, pointing dogs (but never retrievers or spaniels, curiously) are often put on tie-out chains, giving them a chance to stretch their legs, take care of personal business, and simply enjoy a change of scenery (pointer puppies).

Kids and puppies are a match made in heaven, each helping the other to become better socialized and more empathetic—even if few kids, to paraphrase the famous Robert Benchley remark, learn to circle three times before going to sleep (Labrador retriever puppies).

Pointer.

Living was easy, and the hot flame of desire that drove them to find and retrieve game—no matter how punishing the conditions—guttered out.

There's perhaps a germ of truth in this. Dogs that live indoors—because they typically get table scraps and other goodies, in addition to their regular food— are more prone to become *literally* soft—which is to say, fat—than dogs kenneled outside. It's worth noting here that the breed statistically most prone to obesity is the Labrador retriever—although physiological factors relating to the Lab's weatherproofing, not to mention its all-but-insatiable appetite, contribute to this tendency as well.

Not surprisingly, an overweight hunting dog has as big a disadvantage as any other overweight athlete. It won't have the stamina, the speed, or the style of its fitter counterparts; it won't be able to go as far, as fast, or as long; it will be at greater risk for injury, illness, and, in particular, exertion-related afflictions like heatstroke. The combination of overweight, out-of-shape dogs and unseasonably high temperatures resulted in catastrophe a few years ago in South Dakota, where an estimated one-hundred-plus dogs succumbed to heat-related illnesses on opening weekend of the pheasant season.

As an aside, I sometimes wonder if a dog that's a little on the thin side might not feel—at an unconscious, almost cellular level—an added sense of urgency, and if that might not make him more focused and "keen," as the Brits say. This is one of the bedrock principles of falconry: falconers regulate the weight of their birds in the most minute increments (to the gram, essentially), for a bird that's overweight will hunt half-heartedly. It will be

If blood and breeding provide the raw material, training is the process that refines, molds, and polishes this raw material into a usable, functional product (English setters).

It's as much an art as it is a science, and for all our advanced understanding of canine psychology and the principles of behavior modification there's still no substitute for patience, persistence, and sound judgment (black Lab).

Knowing when to stop (or at least slow down), knowing when the dog's ready for the next step, knowing when a correction is indicated: These are questions every trainer faces, questions to which the answers are rarely cut-and-dried (black Lab).

In the words of one eminent pro, "The most important thing in dog training is what you *don't* do" (black Lab).

The goal, always, is for the training to "disappear," for everything the dog does to appear natural, spontaneous, and unscripted (yellow Labs).

As the legendary pointer breeder Robert G. Wehle liked to put it, the mark of a skilled trainer is that he "leaves no fingerprints" (black Labs).

Bob Wehle also made what may be the single wisest observation ever on the topic: "The actual mechanics of training are quite simple. The difficult and important part is how the mechanics are carried out and what you have left when the job is done" (black Lab).

slack-mettled—to use another evocative Anglicism—for the simple reason that it isn't hungry and therefore lacks incentive.

Given the close association between falconry and the sporting breeds—many of which were originally developed for falconry purposes (the pointing breeds in particular)—I have a hunch that whether bird dogs respond the same way or not, historically a lot of their masters took it as an article of faith that their dogs should be kept a little hungry (although not to the degree that they became physically weak, obviously). This belief is still prevalent among houndsmen, but then, hound folk are a little, well, *different*. Clearly a hungry wolf is a more tenacious, more committed hunter than a well-fed one. And you know what they say: Scratch a dog, find a wolf. After all, wolves and dogs share 99.8 percent of the same DNA, and the thing that impels them both to hunt—what ethologists call prey chase drive—is the same as well. In the sporting breeds, we've refined and selectively directed this drive, but at its molten core, it's still what it's always been: one of the basic expressions of the survival instinct itself.

So when our dogs hunt with such intensity and furious purpose that it's as if their lives depended on it, it's because deep in their ancient predator's soul a part of them is convinced that it *does*.

BEDFELLOWS, STRANGE OR OTHERWISE

Issues of health and cleanliness also fed the conviction that dogs should be kenneled away from human domiciles. For as long as there have been dogs,

> "I do not believe any man and dog can really know each other thoroughly unless they sleep together for some time."
>
> —John Sergeant Wise

there have been dogs with fleas—and it's only been within the comparatively recent past that we've had effective repellants for them. Hence the old proverb, Lie down with dogs, and you'll wake up with fleas. Mange was a concern as well, along with a host of other parasites and diseases.

If you're thinking, "Wait a minute—most diseases of dogs can't be transmitted to humans," you're absolutely right. But what you have to remember

Irish and Red setters

With its classic lines, elegant proportions, and lustrous mahogany coat, the Irish setter is among the most regally handsome—and immediately recognizable—of the sporting dogs. But such beauty has a price, and for many years the breed languished as a hunter. During the last half-century, its hunting qualities have been restored. There is no universally agreed upon definition of Red setter, but many use the term to refer to dogs that trace back to the English setter outcrosses made in the 1950s that helped bring back the breed as a top-notch gun dog.

Weimaraner

No sporting breed has ever received the kind of hype the "Gray Ghost" did in the 1950s—and no breed has suffered as much from it. Touted as a wonder dog that would do everything but mix your post-hunt martinis and clean, stuff, and roast your birds, it couldn't possibly live up to expectations. As a result, it rarely got the credit it deserved for what it did bring to the table. This is beginning to change, the Weimaraner's skill set being very similar to the German shorthair's—although the ubiquitous popularity of William Wegman's photographs of the breed may not be an altogether positive development.

is that, for all but a sliver of our shared history (15,000 years, minimum), humans didn't know that. And perhaps the most dreaded disease of all, rabies, which is incurable and invariably accompanied by a horrifying descent into madness, was highly transmittable—and the most common vector was the bite of an afflicted dog.

Still, there have always been hunters who've flouted convention and shared their quarters, and even their sleeping arrangements, with their dogs. The rock band Three Dog Night took its name from an aboriginal term for an especially chilly evening—that is, a night made tolerable only by the body heat of three dogs sleeping beside you. The artist George Catlin, who traveled among the Plains Indians in the 1830s, reported, "Among all Indian tribes the dog is more valued than among any part of the civilized world. They hunt together and are equal sharers in the chase. Their bed is one."

ROYAL BLOOD

More recently, it's not merely a coincidence that so many dogs whose names are hallowed in field trial circles—and whose blood has contributed mightily to the development of their respective breeds—have been the day-in, day-out companions of the men who trained and handled them.

Just as dog shows are essentially conformation competitions—beauty pageants, if you will—field trials are *performance* competitions. The pointing breeds are expected to find and point birds; the flushing breeds (springer and cocker spaniels, primarily) are expected to find and flush birds (put them to wing, that is); and the retrieving breeds are expected to find and retrieve birds. The dogs that do these things best—the ones that display the most style, energy, and charisma, make the fewest mistakes, and require the least amount of assistance from their human handler—are declared the winners. That's an incredible generalization (so much so that I cringe a little at having written it), but it gives you the basic idea.

> Field trials provide a yardstick for the objective evaluation of breeding stock.

Each of these three major groups (pointing, flushing, retrieving) is further subdivided into a dizzying array of what are known as specialty stakes. Dogs up to about one year of age, for example, typically compete in puppy stakes, while those between one and two years of age compete in derby stakes. Trials for adult dogs are called all-age stakes. Some stakes are open, meaning they're open to professional trainers as well as amateurs, while others,

Golden retriever.

designated amateur, are restricted to amateur handlers only—usually (but not always) the person who owns the dog.

While there are a few additional wrinkles in the flushing and retrieving categories, the permutations of pointing dog trials are seemingly endless. This is a reflection not only of the widely different hunting styles the various

Field trials and hunt tests are often touted as ways to extend the hunting season and spend more time afield with your dog (Chesapeake Bay retriever).

These days, though, a lot of folks who compete in these events view them as ends in themselves and treat hunting as a sideline (. . . if they hunt at all: at the highest levels of field trial competition, many of the participants don't hunt, or, if they do, they use different dogs than the ones they run in trials).

Golden retrievers.

Field trials are social events, too. They become a way of life for many people; the locations may vary from weekend to weekend, but the faces, for the most part, stay the same.

Yellow Lab.

pointing breeds embody but of the widely different habits and habitats of the popular North American gamebirds. Pointing dog trials are the only classification in which a certain percentage are contested on wild (i.e., naturally occurring) game—and what's required of a dog in the claustrophobically thick, brushy cover frequented by woodcock and ruffed grouse in New England is a world away, literally and figuratively, from what's required on the Canadian prairies, with their limitless vistas and scattered coveys of Huns and sharptails.

In any event (although this is also something of a generalization), because field trials provide a yardstick for the objective evaluation of breeding stock, dogs that distinguish themselves in competition tend to be the ones breeders utilize. So it's a pretty safe bet that, even if the closest your dog's ever come to a bird is a pilfered Chicken McNugget, the blood of champions courses through its veins.

LIKE FOLKS

When the famed professional trainer Earl Crangle was starting out in the early 1940s, he had only two dogs in his field trial string: the pointer Tarheelia's Lucky Strike and the English setter Hillbright Susanna. As Earl used to put it in his homespun way, "We lived together, like folks." Strike and Susanna slept in Earl's house at night; when he was on the road they stayed with him in his motel. An almost mystical rapport developed between them, a rapport that gave rise to great mutual trust and confidence and translated into stirring field trial victories from the prairies of Canada to the piney

Golden retriever as pillow.

woods of Georgia, on game that ranged from sharp-tailed grouse to pheasants to bobwhite quail.

For two seasons they set the field trial world ablaze, but then Earl, although an American citizen, finagled his way into the Royal Canadian Air Force. (This was before the United States entered World War II.) He turned Strike and Susanna over to his father, George, a highly regarded trainer in his

While it's important to allow your dog the freedom to do the job its breeding, training, and instincts have equipped it to do—not to over-control it, in other words—it's equally important that you be a good field manager, ever-mindful of your dog's condition and vigilant to any signs that it is laboring. Pausing for a cool drink and a few minutes' rest never hurts—and sometimes that makes all the difference (yellow Lab).

At the end of the day, it's altogether fitting for a hunter and his dog to share a reflective moment, to take pride in having done their jobs well, and to bask in the satisfying glow of their accomplishments—although one of the measures of a true dog man (or woman) is that he always values the performance of his four-legged partner more highly than his own. (Facing page top: German wirehair pointer. Bottom right and left: black Labs.)

English setters.

Black Lab.

Everybody loves his or her dog—but when the dog and the person are hunting partners, their relationship has a depth, strength, and mutuality that make it unique.

Chocolate Lab.

own right but one who had a large string of field trial dogs and therefore couldn't give them the kind of personal attention Earl had. It took both dogs some time to adapt, Susanna especially, as setters, more so than pointers, tend to need an intimate bond with their handler in order to perform at their best—and, in particular, to strike the fine balance between subservience and boldness that wins field trial championships. While Earl went on to compile a fine record after he returned from the war—Strike even appeared on the cover of *Life* magazine (what different times those were!)—he never achieved quite the same level of success he'd enjoyed when it was just the three of them, "like folks."

> An almost mystical rapport developed between them, giving rise to great mutual trust and confidence.

Golden Retriever

The golden is the original party animal, as eager to sniff out a good time as it is a skulking pheasant. Its ebullience is contagious: there's nothing like a golden to chase away the blues, to purge the soul of all that is sullen, dour, and grumpy. And while the golden's beauty and balletic grace go without saying, don't be fooled. This is one brainy blonde, capable of the most demanding service dog work and of performing at the highest levels in field trial competition. True, goldens shed like crazy, but what's a little dog hair between friends?

Another English setter immortal, Johnny Crockett—the last of his breed to win the National Championship for all age quail dogs at Grand Junction, Tennessee (a feat he accomplished in 1970)—was for all intents and purposes the house pet of his trainer, W.C. Kirk, and his family. I recall reading that Johnny, who weighed thirty-eight pounds soaking wet and had a friendly wag of the tail for everyone he met, would pull the Kirks' young son around in a little red wagon, and that his favorite place to curl up for a nap was beneath the TV set. Yet this was a dog whose grit, courage, and desire to find game were the stuff of legend, a dog that would have braved the fires of hell to point a covey of quail.

He may have lived in comparative comfort, but he was as tough as they come.

FORGING A BOND

Setters, as noted, seem to profit more from this kind of intimate relationship with people than pointers do, especially in the crucible of field trial competition. The demands imposed by championship-level field trials are extreme; to be successful, a dog not only has to conquer the considerable physical challenges but must maintain its poise—and remember its training—in the face of the most intense distractions. As with any world-class athlete, confidence and mental toughness are just as important as raw talent. To develop these traits, setters typically need a much more personal, hands-on training program than pointers, which tend to be tough and independent from the get-go.

This is one of the big reasons professional field trial handlers prefer pointers: they're more amenable to "mass-production," as it were. A similar dynamic explains why retriever trainers typically prefer Labs to goldens. As a prominent trainer once explained it to me, "Goldens tend to be thinkers; Labs tend to be *doers.*" But there are examples from virtually every sporting breed of

A dog that's developed a strong bond with its handler will better understand what's expected of it.

highly accomplished dogs that rarely leave the sides of their masters. One of the top German shorthaired pointers in America as this is being written,

Golden retriever and Weimaraner.

Echo's Little Bit of Clown, is the boon companion of her trainer/handler, Ray Dohse. Get Ray on the phone, either at home or on his cell, and chances are that "Bitty" is within earshot. When Ray's on the road—and as a field trial handler he's on the road a lot—Bitty's right next to him, on the front seat of the truck.

The thing is, these dogs may have it soft—but they don't play it that way. I'm reminded of an old field trial adage that goes, "Beware the man with one dog." It's not so much that the one-dog man is able to focus all his training time, energy, and talent on just one dog (although that's part of it, too) but that the constancy and exclusivity of the relationship creates such a profound and powerful attachment—a *bond*, to use a word much in vogue these days in dog training circles.

A dog that's developed a strong bond with its handler will not only better understand what's expected of it, but because the dog's desire to please this

Labrador Retriever

Intelligent, trainable, and even-tempered; calm and relaxed or enthusiastic and intense, as the occasion requires; robustly athletic and broadly talented; great with kids and wonderful with the elderly, infirm, and disabled; a terrific hunter to boot: is it any wonder that the Lab is far and away the most popular breed in America? If your assignment was to create a blueprint for the perfect dog, the result would look an awful lot like the Labrador retriever. It even comes in a choice of colors.

REINFORCING THE BOND

While few hunters put such a bottom-line spin on it, time spent with your dog in any situation or circumstance is always profitable. Not only does it reinforce the bond—thus fostering biddability and that elusive quality known as *eagerness to please*—it also helps both of you learn to read each other's body language and anticipate each other's moves. This is an instance in which familiarity emphatically does *not* breed contempt (Labs and golden retrievers).

PARTNERING WITH
THEIR PEOPLE

All dogs relish the chance to hang out with their human family (their pack, essentially)—and none more so than the sporting breeds, which for hundreds of years have been bred to work with people, to partner with them.

Simply put, they are the ultimate people dogs, adaptable to any environment or setting and truly "happy to be here"—wherever here happens to be.

They're always good company, too: patient, understanding, rarely critical, and unfailingly supportive of the day's program—as long as they're included, that is.

Gordon Setter

Perhaps the ultimate choice for the sportsman who values tradition, the Gordon setter, like the Irish, has suffered for its beauty. Prized by nineteenth-century market hunters for its reliability and stamina, the "black and tan" fell out of favor as faster, wider-ranging dogs became the vogue. And as its breeding was increasingly co-opted by show interests, true working Gordons became a rarity. But there were always a few if you knew where to look, and with the world now at your fingertips—literally—finding a quality, field-bred Gordon is easier than ever.

position to "optimize" its potential. You won't make a silk purse out of a sow's ear—but you'll have the prettiest darn sow's ear anyone ever saw.

And should you ever need your dog to help you out of a tight spot—or maybe even tow you to shore through freezing water—well, at least you'll have loaded the dice in your favor.

THE BETTER PART OF OURSELVES

The other side of this coin is that these dogs are terrifically enjoyable to be around, so why would we want to deprive ourselves of the myriad pleasures of their company? Our dogs amuse and entertain, uplift and inspire, calm and reassure us. The nudge of a cold nose, the thump of a tail on the floor, the insistent press of a tennis ball against your hand: they never fail to give us what we need, when we need it.

Exercise is as important to a dog's health and sense of well-being as it is to ours, so it makes sense to kill two birds with one stone and recruit your dog as your work-out buddy. Chances are you'll get very little resistance to this suggestion (golden retriever). Walking puppies—exposing them to different environments and getting them used to the whole wide world of sights, scents, sounds, and critters—is beneficial on so many levels that you could hardly list them all. It's a crucial step toward getting them started on the right path—and it lets you fulfill that childhood fantasy of playing the Pied Piper of Hamlin, too (Lab puppies).

Sitting at opposite ends of a canoe can put even the most bombproof relationship to the test, but for a hunter and dog that have weathered the storms and traveled the miles, it's smooth sailing all the way (yellow Lab). There are times when a touch and a glance say everything that needs to be said, and words would only get in the way (golden retriever).

COMMON PURPOSE AND SHARED DESIRE

It's the oldest, most enduring partnership: dogs and
men, hunting. A well-trained
dog will put more birds in
your bag, but it's ultimately
the intangibles that dogs
bring to the party—their
passion and panache, their
intensity, enthusiasm, and
style—that are the more
lasting and irreplaceable
part of their contribution.

A woman's face may have launched a
thousand ships, but the dreams that have
set sail on the backs of bird dog puppies
are beyond counting.

Joined in common purpose and driven
by shared desire, the hunter and his dog
complement each other's strengths, and
compensate for each other's weaknesses.

Labs and golden retrievers.

They teach us lessons, too: in loyalty, generosity, and equanimity; in responsiveness to the needs of others and willingness to give without expectation of return; in the desire to make the most of every opportunity and the humility to be grateful for all the good things that come your way. Indeed, their example often shames us; when we look at our dogs, we see the qualities we wish we possessed, the purity and nobility we aspire to. We see the better part of ourselves.

They enrich our lives immeasurably, and they make us happier, healthier people. Dogs have a stabilizing influence, helping us cope with stressful situations, reducing our feelings of anxiety, deflecting the inclination toward depression. In short, they help keep us sane.

Which is not to say they can't be royal pains in the ass sometimes. They'll test your patience, to be sure—and not just as puppies, when a certain amount of chewing, peeing, tipping things over, and what might be called *random destruction* are simply the dues you pay, the price of admission to the club. Even a dog that knows better will occasionally let its baser impulses get the upper hand. Food left within easy reach—a juicy burger, for example—is invariably sorely tempting, but the topper in this category for me will always be the number that a yellow Lab named Fred did to his master's high-grade Browning Superposed, his jaws working like a reciprocating engine as they mashed the fancy walnut stock to a lumpy pulp.

What possessed Fred to do this has been the subject of endless speculation,

Our dogs amuse and entertain

Perhaps because we project so many human qualities onto them, dogs have an almost infinite capacity for keeping us amused. (As for cats, well, the less said of them, the better.) And in these parlous times, the value of a little comic relief—as provided by this somewhat perplexed English setter—should not be underestimated.

Uplift and inspire, calm and assure us

Whether it's a lick, a nudge, a proffered paw, or a thump of the tail, dogs always seem to know just what we need. Their timing's perfect, too. And anyone who can hold a puppy and not feel the weight of his or her burdens suddenly lifted is made of something other than flesh and blood.

Golden retriever puppies.

They teach us lessons

The moral here is clear: don't stick your nose in where it doesn't belong.

German wirehair pointer with porcupine quills in nose.

Loyalty, generosity, and equanimity

Many people know the story of Greyfriars Bobby, the Skye terrier that stayed by his master's grave in nineteenth-century Edinburgh, Scotland, day and night for fourteen years—leaving only to beg an occasional meal. Let's hope the name of this Lab, while faithful in his own right, achieves no similar distinction (black Lab).

The desire to make the most of every opportunity

The Roman dictum carpe diem—Seize the day!—might have been coined with dogs in mind. You never need to tell them twice; that's for sure (golden retriever puppies).

The humility to be grateful for all the good things that come your way

No matter how small the kindness or insignificant the gesture, your dog will notice it—and be grateful. In their eyes, you—meaning your presence, your approval, and, yes, your love—are the greatest gift they can ever receive. If that doesn't humble you and inspire you to do the best you can by your dog, well, it ought to (black Lab).

but no conclusive answer has emerged. At least he, unlike the gunstock, survived; those of us present when Fred's owner discovered his "handiwork" can attest that it was touch-and-go there for awhile.

PARTNERS

Any dog is better than no dog, but while there's something to admire about every breed (in theory, anyway, for if put to the wall, I'd be hard-pressed to mount much of a defense for the ankle-biting varieties I collectively refer to as little yappy dogs), I honestly believe that the sporting breeds make the finest companions. Apparently a lot of people are of this same opinion: the Labrador retriever has been the most popular breed in America for a number of years now, with the golden retriever currently running second. A distant second, true, but second nevertheless.

The thing that the Lab, the golden, and the rest of the sporting breeds bring to the party is that they've been bred continuously, over many generations, to work with people, to *partner* with them. They don't merely have to run fast, or fit in a starlet's purse, or pose attractively at the end of a leash. They have to *do a job*, a job that requires a diverse set of physical skills and, even more important, demands a high degree of mental aptitude coupled with basic psychological and emotional soundness. In other words, the sporting breeds have to be intelligent, trainable, resilient, eager to please, even-tempered, and, if not necessarily sweet-natured, at least of a tolerant and generally agreeable bent.

Any dog is better than no dog.

Another quality shared by many of the sporting breeds is their classification by behavioral scientists as low fear and low aggression. Usually a dog deemed high in one of these characteristics will be low in the other, and

Does this remind anyone else of an Oreo cookie with fudge in the center? (Three Lab puppies.)

English setters.

Gunner, dog, and bird: together they are the essential trinity of upland hunting, each defined by the other and made incomplete by the absence of one. When everything else is stripped away, the desire to hunt and find game remains the glowing ember at the heart of it all.

Approaching a point is one of the most dramatic, expectant acts in the realm of outdoor sports. Your heart pounds, your mouth goes cottony, you struggle to stay cool and focused. Sometimes, you even succeed.

It's not just intelligence that you see in a Labrador's eyes, it's perceptiveness, comprehension, understanding. They're not just smart; they're *scary* smart (yellow Lab).

Lab's intelligence, of course, is an acknowledged marvel; as early as 1861, one Lambert de Boilieu observed, "The Labrador retriever, let me remark, is a bold fellow, and, when well taught, understands, almost as well as any Christian biped, what you say to him."

YELLOW LABS

Almost human is a term Lab people use a lot. Even fans of other breeds, when put to the wall, have to admit that Labs have a certain something, a *je ne sais quoi* that sets them apart—and puppies have it most of all.

Another thing the Lab has going for it is an exceptional working memory, which enables it to store and recall images for future use—where the ducks fell, for instance. This helps explain why the Lab is such a quick study, absorbing and remembering its lessons at a rate guaranteed to make it the teacher's pet. Labs are also blessed with remarkably keen eyesight—a function, again, of being bred to mark where downed birds fall. While most dogs see at about a 20/70 level, the eyesight of Labs is thought to be closer to the human

The Lab's intelligence, of course, is an acknowledged marvel.

20/20 benchmark. This begs the question, if the world Labs see looks more like the world *we* see, is it really any wonder that we feel such a tremendous affinity with them?

It's likely that the visual acuity of goldens is better than average, too (although all dogs primarily "see" with their noses), and, in fact, goldens rank very close to Labs in pretty much all the aforementioned mental and psychological categories. So it's no surprise, then, that the golden is number two in overall popularity, or that it's also among the best choices for guide and service work. Here in Green Bay, there was a heartwarming story recently about a woman with cerebral palsy who'd fallen in the road outside her apartment complex, couldn't get up, and was in real danger of being hit by a car.

Fortunately, her golden retriever service dog, by barking furiously outside the door, was able to summon help and lead them to her location.

ETERNALLY PLAYFUL

Of course, these same qualities are the reasons that Labs, goldens, and the rest of the sporting breeds make such terrific family dogs—and in particular why they're so good with children. They're tolerant, affectionate, and—something I haven't mentioned yet—they typically love to play. This brings up the phenomenon of *neoteny*, which refers to the retention of juvenile characteristics into adulthood. Most ethologists believe that neoteny is the crucial wedge that allowed the dog to split off from the wolf, be domesticated by Stone Age humans, and literally *become* the dog. While the circuitry of post-adolescent wolves ossifies, locking them into certain patterns of behavior, dogs, because of their neotenized brains, remain behaviorally "plastic": malleable, adaptable, receptive to new tricks, eminently trainable, and eternally playful. In a sense, every dog—every Lab, golden, and Chessie; every pointer, setter, and Brittany; every cocker, springer, and Clumber—is a puppy in an adult's body.

> Dog brains remain malleable, adaptable, receptive to new tricks, eminently trainable and eternally playful.

Neoteny also helps explain why our dogs lap up—and dish out—so much affection. Just as the wolf puppy has a deeply rooted need for affirmation and positive reinforcement from its superiors in the hierarchy of the pack, the dog, throughout its life, craves the attention and approval of the human family that comprises its "pack." Feeling loved, and that it belongs, are essential

Golden retrievers.

to the dog's sense of well-being—although some dogs, and some breeds, tend

to be more needy, or more stoic, in this respect than others.

FUNCTION FIRST

Ultimately, the sterling qualities that make the sporting breeds the royalty of

dogdom exist because they serve a purpose, because they promote *function*.

And whether we hunt with our dogs or not, it's critically important that we

recognize this. When a breed's functional qualities—the pointing and retriev-

ing instincts, the stamina and athleticism to perform capably in the field, the

intelligence to take training, etc.—are neglected and puppies are produced

simply to satisfy the demands of the marketplace, the result, within a shockingly

Golden retriever.

The writer, sportsman, and dog authority Robert F. Jones always maintained that one of the real secrets to training was taking advantage of the dog's essential playfulness—its "need to play," as he put it. You don't have to be a genius—or even a Dog Whisperer—to see why this approach would work. Another strategy that pays big dividends is peer pressure. Dogs are competitive by nature (which is why they always want the other dog's food, even if it's exactly the same as theirs). Canny trainers know how to use this to mold desirable behaviors without a dog even realizing it.

Labrador retrievers.

SERIOUS PLAY, PLAYFUL WORK

Hunting is a serious business and one that places terrific demands on a dog. We expect them to do very "grown-up" things, which is why it can be easy to forget that beneath their adult exterior is a part of them that never grows up. It's what makes dogs dogs and distinguishes them from wolves. And it's why, no matter how undeserving we may be, they will always look up to us.

Springer spaniel adults and puppy.

Every dog is
a puppy in an
adult's body.

few generations, is a corruption. It may look the same, but it won't *be* the same.

This is the danger whenever a breed becomes wildly popular; the puppy mills ramp up, dogs are bred without any regard to their physical or psychological soundness, and the patient, devoted work of breeders who were guided not by thoughts of profit or personal gain, but by an abiding vision of excellence, is undone. It happened in the early twentieth century with the Irish setter: bred strictly for beauty, it lost the brains, bird sense, and rugged constitution that had once made it a favorite of discriminating bird hunters. And that may well happen again today with the Lab and the golden.

Pull one thread, and the whole fabric unravels.

So, admire the form—but above all, exalt the function. Without that, they're just dogs. And remember the words of William Henry Herbert, who under the *nom de plume* Frank Forester in the mid-nineteenth century was perhaps the first person on American soil to write knowledgeably about these breeds we love with such fierce, abiding passion:

> After the gun or rifle, the great essential as to the mere killing of game is his dog to the sportsman; but when we regard him as the living, the intelligent, the more than half-reasoning companion, the docile, obedient, enduring, uncomplaining servant, the faithful, grateful, submissive, affectionate friend, and not unseldom the last mourner of the dead master, unmourned by all beside … we must think of him as something widely different from the tool of wood and iron.

From sixty to zero in the blink of an eye: when a pointer hits scent, it's as if he's slammed into an invisible wall. (English setter and pointer on point.)

The sterling qualities that make the sporting breeds
the royalty of dogdom exist because they serve a purpose.

BIRDS ARE WHERE YOU FIND 'EM

The classic, high-on-both-ends style that you see in magazines and calendars is at best a partial reflection of reality. There's an old saying that goes "Birds are where you find 'em." Often as not this translates to the kind of brushy, tangled places that force a pointing dog to become a contortionist. Too many hunters go into hurry-up mode when their dog locks up on point—all but sprinting to get to their dog and flush the birds. Not that you should dawdle, mind you, but assuming your dog's reliably staunch there's no need to rush. Take a moment, soak it all in, and let the scene etch itself on your memory.

Just so everybody's clear on this: pointing dogs don't invariably raise one forepaw—although that's certainly what most people see in their mind's eye when they picture a dog on point. It depends on the individual dog, the way it responds to scent, and its interpretation of the signals the scent is sending (e.g., "Don't move a muscle," or, "It's OK to ease up a little closer).

Reading the body language of a dog on point is a skill that experience teaches, that all good hunters learn, and that appears as mystical as the divination of omens to the uninitiated. Some sportsmen can, from a certain tilt of the tail or cant of the head, even tell which species of bird their dog's pointing (left, English setter; all others pointers).

A persistent topic of debate in the pointing dog camp is whether a dog should break point on its own recognizance and "self-relocate" when it knows the birds are running, or whether it should stay on point until released by its handler. Most really experienced hunters—the ones with tattered vests, scars on the backs of their hands, and guns with most of the bluing worn off the barrels—come down on the side of self-relocation. Like so much else in the gunner-gun dog partnership, it's a matter of trust.

Upland bird hunting means walking, and because it is the "natural condition of game to be scarce," as the philosopher Ortega y Gasset observed, there are times when you put in a lot of miles between birds. So you might as well have a dog whose style of running—on the ground, to use the bird dog term—is pleasing to the eye (English setter).

And because it is the natural condition of the human mind to daydream, your mind wanders. Nothing galvanizes your attention and brings you back to the here and now more quickly, however, than a dog on point (English setter).

Black Lab.

Honoring another dog's point—often called backing (short for backpointing)—is something that all pointing dogs should do. It comes naturally to some (dogs have been known to back rocks, stumps, boxes, and just about anything else that's roughly the size, shape, and color of a dog on point), but others have to be trained to do it. With certain breeds, and certain incorrigible individuals, teaching them to back can be like getting a kid to eat vegetables. Desire manifests itself in different ways with different breeds, but ultimately it flows from the same source: the prey drive. When a Lab goes for a retrieve with such ferocity of purpose that it's as if its life depends on it, that's because—at an almost cellular level—a part of the dog is convinced its life does depend on it.

There is a time for every purpose under heaven—and even the keenest hunter needs, and deserves, a little R&R (Weimaraner).

In the Woods, Fields, and Marshes

::

HARD LESSONS ON THE HUNTER'S ROAD

If you don't count the time my normally unflappable dad almost stepped on a hen pheasant, lost his footing, and—to the enduring amusement of our companions—fell ass-over-teakettle onto the concrete-hard ground, my first real hunt with bird dogs was stunningly uneventful. It was late December, in the twilight of the Iowa season; the landscape was reduced to its wintry, monochromatic essence—browns, off-whites, shades of gray—the few surviving roosters so wild and wary as to be all but unapproachable.

Chocolate Labrador in marsh.

There are all sorts of reasons we hunt with dogs, many of which have precious little to do with putting more birds in the freezer. With respect to waterfowl hunting, one of the big reasons is ethical. An estimated 25 percent of the ducks and geese shot by hunters go unrecovered; but this percentage drops precipitously among sportsmen who use retrievers. It's the right thing to do, and it's the good thing to do (black Lab with hunter and goose decoys at sunrise).

Dove hunting is a waiting game, but when the birds come—and come they will—the action's fast and furious and the shooting's some of the most challenging there is. Even a top gun can expect to burn a box of shells per ten doves.

A reliable "pick-up dog" helps ensure that none of your hard-earned rewards go unreaped.

The wonderful writer Robert F. Jones observed that, "the essence of American upland bird hunting is a long hard walk through tough cover," usually in the company of "a dog who is also a friend." No one ever said it better.

Lab retrievers in Montana.

SIFTING THE BREEZE

It's a miracle, really, the way a dog's nose can divine the scent of a single bird in a sea of grass, the hidden thing at the heart of it all (English setter, right). There is no way we can really comprehend what a dog smells, or what its nose reveals to that dog, except to think of it in terms of our own sense of sight. In other words, dogs see with their noses. Pointing dogs provide the clearest illustration of this; while at times they appear to be "looking" at the bird, in fact they're focusing on the source of the scent. (It's very rare—although it does happen—for them to actually see a bird on the ground.) At other times, and especially in open country, their nose will be tilted upward as they literally sift the breeze for molecules of scent, as brilliant and distinct as stars (English setter and pointer on point, below).

When they're in the blind, retrievers rely more on their eyes and ears; every seasoned water-fowler has had the experience of noticing his dog suddenly snap to attention, its eyes burning a hole in a sharply defined, but apparently empty, patch of sky—a patch of sky from which, moments later, a flock of ducks emerges. But once the birds start falling, the retriever's nose is every bit as indispensable to the job as the pointing dog's is (golden retriever, left; all others, black Labs).

Quail are small, they fly fast—and a 16-gauge pumpgun with a modified choke (a Winchester Model 12, in case you're wondering) is not the implement of choice for them.

I was going to write that this was the day my eyes were opened, the day I saw what dogs are truly capable of—their near-miraculous feats of athleticism, tenacity, and olfactory prowess. But that wouldn't be quite right. Instead, it was the day when what I saw in the field merged with the vision I'd formed in my mind, when what I experienced merged with what I'd dreamed. It was the day when the magic of dogs making game—magic I'd known only from the pages of books like *Big Red, Wing & Shot,* and *Algonquin* (to name only the most affecting) but which I believed in with all my heart and soul and desperately wanted to touch and feel and be a part of—was revealed to me and proven to

Chesapeake Bay Retriever

One of the few breeds that originated in North America, the Chessie has long been the retriever of choice among hard-core waterfowlers. Seemingly impervious to cold, the Chessie is an amphibious tank, breaking ice, bucking treacherous currents, going to whatever extremes are necessary in order to bring back its duck. Chesapeakes tend to be deeply attached to their masters (sometimes overprotectively so) and, by the same token, to regard the rest of humanity with gimlet-eyed suspicion. Whether this is a knock on the breed or a selling point continues to be debated.

Hunting with a dog speaks to your values and priorities, to the things that are important in your experience of the outdoors and the things that are not. It also speaks to your tastes and points up the fact that hunting with a dog is an aesthetic choice as much as it is a functional one. Dogs of course are not machines. Even the best ones make mistakes—and sometimes the

birds simply win. It's not as if they want to be found, after all. To paraphrase an observation made by the revered George Bird Evans, one lives more richly because of one's dogs, but at the risk of living more miserably. At its best, though, when your dog does its part and you do yours, bird hunting becomes a thing of transcendent beauty, a glorious

dance performed on nature's stage. It's for these days, even slivers of days, that we live. They are what sustain us, their memory and their possibility. Without a dog, you're just going through the motions. It feels as hollow as an empty shell.

Facing page, top, Lab; bottom right, English setter.

This page top, Lab; middle, German wirehair pointer.

A PRACTICAL CHOICE: HUNTING WITH A DOG

The idea of hunting ruffed grouse and woodcock without a dog is as unthinkable as the idea of French cuisine without fine wine. It isn't really hunting; it's just walking in the woods. The English setter is the traditional choice for ruffed grouse hunting; whether it's the best choice is really beside the point. Style matters, too.

At the end of a day in the autumn woods, men and dogs alike are suffused with a kind of weary contentment—and the number of birds in the bag has precious little to do with it.

Dispensing the occasional snack builds rapport and reinforces the bond between gunner and dog. It's also the case that bird hunters of both the two- and four-legged varieties, like armies, march on their stomachs.

Behind the rough-hewn façade of every mighty hunter beats the heart of a lap dog. And it never hurts to let your dog know it's welcome there—within reasonable limits, of course.

When dogs and hunters both hold up their end of the partnership, the results can be very, very sweet. As Ortega y Gasset famously—and rightly—observed, "One kills in order to have hunted."

exist as a tangible presence in the world. I have been in thrall to it irresistibly ever since, its servant and disciple and messenger.

There was something in the air from the day's beginning, an augury of the exalted. Tufts of tawny little bluestem poked out from the snow on the steeper, wind-scoured slopes; the sun seemed to set them ablaze, their glow bathing the entire hillside. The light had the quality of a Vermeer: luminous, immortal. "Look!" I cried, and we turned our heads as one to see an enormous covey of quail come streaming out of the timber, quail that resembled a shower of meteors as they emerged from the shadows and were suddenly illuminated. They pitched in, some diving into the clumps of prairie grass, others seeking the circle of bare earth beneath the dwarf cedars that grew there, so dark as to appear almost black.

The dog's nose is a window onto unseen worlds.

"My God," one of the group exclaimed. "There's forty birds in that covey if there's one!"

Later, when we'd scattered the covey and begun to follow up the singles, I witnessed my first miracle. We'd marked several birds along a grassy crease in a field of picked corn, and as the Brittanys bounded ahead one whirled ninety degrees, mid-stride, and landed on point. Instantly, the other dog honored.

"Go ahead and kick up the bird," someone said, but as I eased in front of the quivering, orange-speckled dogs I saw that the shallow draw had drifted in.

There were a few stems of grass, but not enough cover to hide a sparrow, much less a pear-plump bobwhite quail. *Another false point,* I thought glumly.

That's when the knee-deep powder I was standing in exploded, a reddish-brown projectile I was able (with some difficulty) to identify as a quail roared out, and I went as slack-jawed as I did the time I saw my friend Jim's ravishing older sister naked. I mean, I was no more prepared for this than I would have been to hear a *poof!* and find myself transformed into a newt. Who knew such a thing was possible?

This scenario repeated itself several times—the Britts locking up staunchly and unequivocally, the bird flushing in a glittering cascade of snow—and my mental state gradually changed from uncomprehending confusion to delighted wonder: wonder not only at the quail's tactics (years later I'd learn that ruffed grouse will do the same thing to save their skins, sometimes even spending the night in a "snow roost") but at the dogs' ability to sniff them out regardless. That, to me, was truly mind-boggling; it brought home, in an unforgettable way, the fact that the dog's nose is a window onto unseen worlds, and that the dog itself is a kind of medium, the Rosetta Stone that enables us to bridge the gap between the realms of sight and scent.

I've never gotten over it, and I'm pretty sure I never will.

BIRDS IN THE BAG

In his classic *Meditations on Hunting,* the philosopher Jose Ortega y Gasset crystallized the central paradox of the sport. "One does not hunt in order to kill," he observed. "On the contrary, one kills in order to have hunted."

For many of us who hunt birds with dogs—most of us, I'd daresay—the kill, while necessary, is secondary. "If I couldn't hunt with a dog, I wouldn't hunt at all" is an oft-repeated mantra. And while the glib answer to the question of why we use dogs is that it makes us more "effective," more "successful" hunters, it's not nearly that simple.

Sometimes it's not even true. We've all been on hunts that were ruined, or at least severely

> A well-trained dog is practical conservation personified.

compromised, by dogs that were out of control, ill-trained, ill-mannered, or some combination thereof. If your name happens to be on the collar of such a dog, you're one of the few people inclined to sympathize with the fan who interfered with a catchable foul ball at Wrigley Field a few years ago and cost the Cubs a trip to the World Series.

Still, all else equal, hunting with a well-trained dog of any breed will put more birds in your bag over the long haul than hunting without one. Such a dog (or dogs) will not only produce more birds and create more opportunities to shoot than you could on your own, it will also put a higher percentage of the birds you *do* shoot into your gamebag. Even a bird you clobber can be heartbreakingly difficult to find in heavy cover—doubly so if it's a diminutive quail, woodcock, or snipe (there's a reason for their subdued, "cryptic" plumage)—and no matter how skilled you are with a scattergun not every bird you knock from the sky falls dead. The legendary outdoor writer Nash Buckingham was one of the most renowned wingshots of his era—but he was also the person who famously declared, "The best long-range duck load is a well-trained retriever."

Waterfowlers, in particular, have long recognized the role a dog can play in reducing what are known as *crippling losses*, typically birds that are wounded and not recovered. Some dive, some "sail" a considerable distance, and some, for all we know, slip through a crack in the space-time continuum. It's been estimated that one out of every four ducks and geese shot in North America is lost, and while hard statistics are elusive there's no doubt whatsoever that the use of retrievers—which, amazingly (if not incomprehensibly), only about 20 percent of waterfowl hunters own—would improve that figure substantially. The eminent retriever trainer Joe DeLoia, who's had a hunting camp in the willow-and-wild rice boglands of northwestern Minnesota since 1945, told me that in a recent span of years he and his companions knocked down 731 ducks and geese—728 of which their dogs brought back. To Old School pros like Joe, men with a fierce commitment to conservation and the abiding belief that a well-trained dog is practical conservation personified, numbers like those speak for themselves.

Viewed in this light, the choice to hunt with a dog looks like the *ethical* thing to do—although most of us don't get that high-minded about it.

CHOICES, CHOICES, CHOICES

But then, when you get down to the nitty-gritty, hunting with a dog is all *about* choices, choices that begin long before you've scooped your first pile of poop or replaced your first shredded loafer, to say nothing of collaborating on your first gamebird. The most fundamental of these, of course, is your choice

Yellow Labrador retriever.

of a breed. If you're a hard-core waterfowler, meaning a person who relies on his dog strictly to recover shot birds and not at all to create shooting opportunities, it's pretty cut-and-dried. You're going to be looking at a Labrador, a golden retriever, or possibly a Chesapeake—although if you opt for the last you're obviously the kind of person who boils his clothes in lye, sets his own broken bones, and generally inclines toward doing things the hard way.

At the opposite end of the spectrum stands the bobwhite quail specialist of the Deep South, Texas, and Oklahoma. His focus is almost entirely on the production side, on dogs that will find, point, and "hold" the birds until he arrives to flush and shoot. This arrival is often hastened by some form of conveyance, traditionally a Tennessee walking horse or mule-drawn shooting wagon—but more practically and popularly a customized (dog boxes, shotgun scabbards, etc.) "Mule"-variety ATV or tricked-out 4WD pickup. Because the coveys are apt to be thinly scattered across the landscape, a good quail dog should show its heels, range out, and gobble sizable chunks of country—and to do this it needs to be endowed with terrific speed, stamina, desire, and independence. As another legendary writer, John Madson, observed, you don't really hunt for quail—you hunt for the *dog* that's hunting for quail.

> You don't really hunt for quail—you hunt for the dog that's hunting quail.

Which, overwhelmingly, is likely to be a pointer. It is, quite simply, the definitive quail dog; whenever the words speed, range, and stamina appear in

Boykin Spaniel

If there's one word that describes the Boykin, it's irrepressible. When you're in a room with one of these guys, you always have the feeling that, like a shaken-up bottle of bubbly, it could pop its cork at any moment and start bouncing off the walls. The state dog of South Carolina, the Boykin's a popular choice in the South as a "pickup dog" on dove shoots and plantation-style quail hunts. It's comparatively rare north of the Mason-Dixon line—and if you want to hear an old-time Rebel Yell just tell a Boykin partisan that his breed is merely a southern-fried version of the state dog of Wisconsin, the American water spaniel.

close proximity, the word pointer can't be far behind. (Some people insist on using the term English pointer, but that's a misnomer. The name of the breed is pointer, period.) A handful of individuals of other pointing breeds have the legs, lungs, and "motor" to give the pointers a run for their money, but ultimately they're the exceptions that prove the rule. Watching pointers run, you wonder that they don't set the ground afire, that they don't leave the earth scorched and blackened in their blazing wakes.

> Watching pointers run, you wonder that they don't set the ground afire.

And when they strike point, stopping so suddenly and violently that you recoil in sympathy to the imagined impact, it's as if they've collided with a steel wall. The transformation wrought by scent on a pointer is almost frightening. "Setters, Brittanys, and German shorthairs face quail as if their lives depended on it," wrote Guy de la Valdéne in his paen to the bobwhite quail,

Pointer

Someone described the pointer as, "a life-support system for a nose." That's a bit extreme, but it cuts to an essential truth: the pointer, to a degree unmatched by any other breed, is laser-focused on the task of finding and pointing birds. Its desire in this respect burns so white-hot that you can almost feel the heat radiating from their bodies—which, befitting the pointer's singleness of purpose, are as lean, hard, and finely tuned as a Formula One racecar. Fast? Pointers make even the fleetest members of other breeds look like they're slogging through mud.

Upland bird hunters tend to fall into two categories: those who love pointers (and think all other breeds are hardly worth the breath it takes to mention them), and those who are scared to death of them.

The thing about pointers is that they run . . . and run . . . and run.

Then they run some more, and then they run some more after that.

Pointers being the definitive quail dogs, they've scorched more earth in the Deep South than Sherman's army. There's only one thing that's sure to stop them: bird scent. Bird scent turns them to stone.

the kennel. There has to be room for judgment, intuition, and, yes, emotion; while you don't necessarily have to follow your heart, you ignore its signals at your peril—especially when dogs are involved.

Choosing a gun dog, then, is an act of self-expression, a statement about who we are as sportsmen and about what we value in our experience of the hunt. Few if any of us hunt in order to survive (except in the sense of maintaining our spiritual well-being), and while we all like to put birds in the bag it's hardly the only yardstick by which we measure the success of a day afield, its pleasures and satisfactions. A single sterling piece of dog work can make an otherwise uneventful hunt burn brightly in memory; a thrilling point on a wary ruffed grouse, for example, the bird seemingly transfixed by the force of the dog's presence—"overawed," as they used to say—is a reward unto itself, over and above what transpires at flush and shot.

English Cocker Spaniel

The resurgence of interest in these pint-sized dynamos, whose abilities are out of all proportion to their stature (many cockers retrieve birds nearly as big as they are), is the biggest story in American gun dogs. Fearless, fiery, and with energy to burn, they're up to any challenge, and their compact dimensions are an ideal fit for the sportsman who makes his home in an urban setting. While they'll invariably test you—the devil himself, observed British gun dog authority Keith Erlandson, is partial to cockers—they require surprisingly little training to become productive partners in the field.

CASTING A SPELL

This ability of certain pointing dogs to cast an almost hypnotic spell over their birds brings to mind the oft-told tale of the grouse hunter whose great and trusted dog—usually an English setter but sometimes a pointer, depending on who's telling the story—got separated from him in hilly country and, despite his diligent efforts, was never seen again. (This was in the days before beepers, electronic tracking collars, etc.) Hunting that same country a few years later, the man stumbled over the bones of his beloved dog (he could tell it was his from the collar). Marveling that even in death his dog seemed to be on point, he walked a few yards in front of it—and found the bones of a grouse.

Pointing dogs, English setters in particular, are of course the traditional choices for ruffed grouse and woodcock hunting (flushing dogs weren't so

English Setter

There's something about English setters that—once they get into your blood—makes it awfully hard to muster much enthusiasm for other pointing breeds. Part of the reason is the way they combine matchless style with serious performance; part of the reason is their irresistibly appealing personalities (no breed has more deeply soulful eyes); and part of the reason is, well, a mystique that can't be precisely articulated. It's been said that a good English setter will spoil you for any other dog—and no one who's been lucky enough to own one is likely to disagree with that.

Nothing did more to popularize flushing dogs for North American upland bird hunting than the ring-necked pheasant. In what was essentially a serendipitous discovery, American sportsmen found that the golden and Labrador retrievers—breeds that had been developed in the British Isles to serve as non-slip retrievers on driven shoots—were well suited to the wildly unpredictable nature of the bird and the forbiddingly thick cover it hides out in.

These breeds were also very good at rounding up pheasants that were lightly hit. In America we call these birds cripples, but the British term runner is more apt. A broken-winged rooster pheasant with his legs still under him is a first-ballot candidate for the Fugitive Hall of Fame—and whenever a saber-tailed, dagger-spurred cockbird comes to hand, you feel as if you and your dog have really accomplished something.

American water spaniel, had a limited following among duck hunters in the Upper Midwest.) Oh, there were a handful of Irish and Gordon setters of legitimate field stock, but the breeding of these once-grand gun dogs had already been largely co-opted by the show crowd, who exalted form and ignored function. As a result, the qualities that had made the "reds" and the "black-and-tans" prized hunters in the late-nineteenth century were allowed to erode and atrophy; it's often said that they were "victims of their own beauty."

Certainly some English setters and pointers handled the running ringnecks just fine. But others, bred to satisfy the wide-ranging quail dog standard (which was, and is, also the standard for most pointing dog field trial competition), were out of their element. There was a void, a slot waiting to be filled by a tractable, easy-handling dog of moderate pace and range, a dog with a little less run and more of an inclination to plunge into heavy cover, a dog that could consistently produce these flying dragons for the gun and reliably bring them back once they hit the ground.

German Shorthaired Pointer

Rugged, efficient, and as dependable as they come, the German shorthaired pointer is the pickup truck of gun dogs. It may not be the fastest or the flashiest, but it can carry the load—and it always gets you there. The fact that it's the pointing dog of choice at shooting preserves—where rule number one is, Do No Harm—speaks volumes, too. And while aloof at first blush, beneath the shorthair's cool Teutonic façade beats a warmly affectionate heart.

Nature abhors a vacuum, as they say, and the unmet needs of American sportsmen in the 1920s prompted a steady stream of imports from across the Atlantic—breeds that have been fixtures here for decades but at the time were considered exotic. In the vanguard of the Continental breeds—so-called because of their origins on the European mainland as opposed to the British Isles—were the Brittany spaniel from France (the "spaniel" designation was officially dropped in the 1980s) and the German shorthaired pointer. They caught on quickly with pheasant hunters and soon proved their worth on other gamebirds as well; they tended to work at a much closer range than pointers and English setters, making them more comfortable for a lot of the bird hunting rank-and-file, and in general they were also stronger natural retrievers and better at tracking and corralling wounded game.

German Wirehaired Pointer

Equally at home on land or in water, the German wirehair is versatility personified. It is unsurpassed at tracking down lightly hit birds, and some owners train their dogs to blood track wounded big game animals (deer, for example) as well. You'll often see this breed referred to as Drahthaar or Deutsch Drahthaar, and while that's linguistically correct (German wirehair is the literal translation of Deutsch Drahthaar), there are some who insist that the AKC-registered German wirehair is an Americanized version, and that only dogs registered with the German parent club deserve to be called Drahthaars.

A working retriever has to be physically rugged and mentally tough. The job demands it: harsh conditions are the norm, and for every retrieve that's a piece of cake there's another that puts all the dog's training, talent, and resolve to the test. Those are the ones you remember, the ones that make the hours of training—the bumpers you threw until your arm ached, the endlessly repetitive drills, the days

when it seemed you'd hit the wall—all worth it. Boldness and compliance are critical parts of the formula, too. Finding the proper balance is an ongoing process, one that requires knowing when to intercede and handle your dog, and knowing when to keep your whistle in your pocket and trust his nose, instincts, and experience to follow the clues and solve the mystery. Handling a retriever is an extended exercise in judgment.

When it all comes together and your dog, swelling with pride, presents you with the bird . . . There's nothing better. Nothing. Moments like these are the reasons we do it, the reasons we study bloodlines and join clubs, the reasons we read books by Quinn and Morgan and Walters, and get up early to drive hundreds of miles to training seminars only to discover a passion and dedication we didn't know we were capable of. But that's the thing about these dogs we hunt with: we may be their trainers, but they are our teachers.

And to have a puppy waiting in the wings, his enthusiasm infectious and his potential unlimited—at least until proven otherwise—well, that's just icing on the cake.

Indeed, many sportsmen were thrilled to discover that these breeds were suitable for light-duty waterfowling in addition to their upland responsibilities. It's for this that they're often described as *versatile breeds*, a term that's become essentially interchangeable with *Continental breeds*. The success of the Brittany and the German shorthair paved the way for other Continentals to become established in North America; the German wirehaired pointer (Drahthaar), which by virtue of its eponymous coat is the best of the versatiles at water work; the Weimaraner, a.k.a. the "Gray Ghost," familiar to many through the widely published images of photographer William Wegman (although it's very rarely encountered in the field); the copper-coated Vizsla, a breed developed on the Magyar Plains of Hungary to point partridges for falconers and their hunting hawks; and the wirehaired pointing griffon, one of the very few breeds whose origins can be traced to a single person, the Dutchman E.K. Korthals.

CHANGING THE GUARD

During this same period, three breeds from Great Britain—breeds that would profoundly affect the American sporting dog scene—began to arrive in numbers here. One of these was the English springer spaniel. Advertised as a pheasant specialist, it was in fact an impeccably credentialed all-purpose hunter—the first choice of the British rough-shooter who pursues a variety of game, both furred and feathered, in the fields, fens, and marshes. The springer brought about a revolution: until its embrace by pheasant hunters (a process that took about as long as it takes to holler "Rooster!"), flushing dogs enjoyed only the tiniest presence on the American stage. There were a few cocker and Clumber spaniels around (they had a limited vogue among wood-cock aficionados in the East and the Mid-Atlantic), but *few* is definitely the operative word. The springer was the breed that, more than any other, popularized (and legitimized) the use of flushing dogs for upland game in the United States and Canada.

Today, of course, with the exception of the bobwhite quail (as noted previously) you'd be hard-pressed to name an upland gamebird that isn't hunted seriously and successfully with flushing dogs, even such unlikely suspects as Hungarian partridge, sharp-tailed grouse, and prairie chickens. One of the most purely enjoyable days of big country hunting I've ever had came on the rolling steppes of North Dakota, courtesy of professional trainer Tom Ness and the two lightning-fast cockers under his direction. The sun was blazing, and

Springer Spaniel

The first flushing dog to have a significant impact on the American sporting scene, the springer was among the wave of British importations in the 1920s that also included the Labrador and golden retrievers. Although originally advertised as a pheasant "specialist"—and while it still stars in that role—it now occupies much the same niche that it does in its native Great Britain: that of the quintessential rough-shooter's dog, capable of handling whatever feathered bounty the countryside offers up.

the birds, sharptails and Huns both, were hunkered in the shade of the plum and chokecherry thickets. When the cockers hit those thickets, it was like guided missiles hitting an ammo dump. The whole world seemed to shudder, roar, and explode.

The other British breeds that found their way to these shores *en masse* in the 1920s were the golden and Labrador retrievers. It hardly seems necessary to remark upon their impact, as they're now the two most popular breeds in America. (Nearly three times as many Labs are registered with the American

My first setter never panned out as a hunter, but she taught me a lot: about dogs, about expectations, about myself.

Kennel Club annually as any other breed.) Both the golden and the Lab were developed to serve as pickup dogs for the shooting parties hosted by assorted Earls, Lords, and Dukes on their magnificent estates; seeking to emulate them, their counterparts among America's landed gentry originally imported these breeds to serve much the same purpose. It was something of a happy accident, in fact, that the Lab and golden were found to have a much broader skill set than merely the ability to retrieve from land. (And land, not water, was their primary milieu in the U.K.; according to retriever authority Richard Wolters, it was said of the early Labs in America that the native Chesapeake Bay retriever "taught them to swim.")

At any rate, shoe-leather bird hunters soon found, to their delight, that goldens and Labs made dandy pheasant dogs: staying close, crashing the thickest cover, putting skulking cockbirds to wing, and bringing back even the liveliest cripples. At the same time (more or less), waterfowlers were learning that these breeds could do just about anything the Chessie could do in a duck blind, and that in addition they were easier to train and handle, less bulky, ponderous, and mulish, and generally more pleasant to be around. In the wag of a tail, the Chesapeake plummeted from top dog in the retriever realm to a very distant third.

PERCHANCE TO DREAM

So if you want to hunt pheasants or damn near any other bird in twenty-first-century America, you have an almost bewildering variety of choices—the proverbial happy dilemma. Some make more sense, on the face of it, than others, but this is not an exercise in logic. Ultimately, hunting with a dog is an act of the imagination, an affirmation of a distinctly human longing: the desire to dream.

Hoping to fulfill their son's dream of having a dog like Big Red, my parents finally bought me an Irish setter (over the gentle protests of friends who were "in the know" and counseled that a Brittany or German shorthair would be a better, safer choice). Sheila never panned out as a hunter, but we had wonderful adventures together, and she taught me a lot—about dogs, about expectations, about myself. The most important thing she taught me, though, is that dogs have a way of making dreams come true—even when they don't.

About Dogs

Hunting and living with gundogs—*partnering* with them in the fullest, most complete sense—is the subject of this book. The dog was the first domesticated animal, after all, and in the preceding chapters we've tried to survey the terrain of this ancient relationship and report on its status in 21st-century America. (Executive Summary: alive, not without its concerns, yet nevertheless brimming with possibilities.) If we've tugged on the heartstrings along the way, well, it's pretty hard to bring up dogs in print or in pictures and be unmoved. Forged in the flames of Stone Age fires, our emotional connection to the dog is so powerful and so profound, that when its measure is revealed to us, it brings us to our knees.

For all its rewards and pleasures, though, this partnership is not to be entered lightly. It's a serious, long-term commitment, with any number of practical considerations that need to be addressed. While the best we can do here is scratch the surface, we thought it might be useful to shine some light on three "issues" that virtually all gundog owners face: picking a puppy, choosing a professional trainer, and getting the most from your older dog. For a more exhaustive discussion of these and other relevant topics, consult *The Ultimate Hunting Dog Reference Book* by Vickie Lamb (The Lyons Press, 2006).

PICKING A PUPPY

From the moment you decide that the time is right to the day you bring home the newest member of the family—from conception to delivery, so to speak—picking a puppy is one of the most engaging and rewarding endeavors you'll ever tackle. It has a little of everything: anticipation, excitement, apprehension (you never know *exactly* what you're getting into), even the thrill of the chase. Think of it as puppy "hunting," and you get the idea.

Like hunting, too, picking a puppy is supremely enjoyable—but it's also serious business. A puppy represents a tremendous commitment of time, money,

Yellow Lab.

energy, and, last but not least, emotional capital. Not just during the first few months, either: Lord willing, that pup is going to be a huge part of your life for the next ten to fifteen years. As they say at the poker table, when you buy a puppy, you go all in.

Your first major decision, obviously, is to settle on a breed. Now, choosing the breed best suited to the birds you hunt and your style of hunting—assuming you care to get that objective about it—is a topic unto itself. It's also way too big to cover here, except to say that if you're still mulling it over, I know a couple books that might help: *The Encyclopedia of North American Sporting Dogs* (Willow Creek Press) and *Gun Dog Breeds* by Charles Fergus (Lyons Press).

On second thought, there's something else I'd like to say. If you opt for an obscure or uncommon breed, you're setting yourself up for a more difficult search than if your choice is, for example, a Labrador, Brittany, or German shorthair. The flip side is that the overall quality of certain less-common breeds—hunting English cockers and field-bred Irish setters come to mind—is probably superior to some of the more popular breeds, so your chances of getting a "keeper" are better.

It comes down to doing your homework and—to invoke a phrase that's become a near-cliché—*picking the right litter*. In other words, find a dedicated, reputable breeder with a solid track record of producing the kind of dog you want and put your trust in him or her to do right by you. That's the really important part, the part where you should focus your efforts and attention.

Once you've done that, picking the individual puppy—assuming it's healthy, happy, alert, inquisitive, and neither noticeably larger nor smaller than its littermates—is largely an exercise in personal preference. The best dog I've ever owned, an English setter named Emmylou, was chosen by my then-wife because, from among a litter of five look-alike females, she had "the sweetest face."

Emmylou's grandson Ernie, a pretty good dog in his own right, was chosen over his littermates because he was the only one who satisfied my predetermined criteria for a white-and-orange male.

The point is, there was nothing "scientific" that led me to choose these particular pups. I was confident in the things that matter: the soundness of the sire and dam, the quality and compatibility of their bloodlines, and the integrity of the breeders. Thinking that you can magically spot the pup that's going to "make it," regardless of the litter's provenance, is like thinking you can catch lightning in a bottle. The fact that a given sire and dam are purebred members of a sporting breed is, by itself, meaningless; unless field-proven dogs are continually bred to field-proven dogs, a phenomenon known as the "drag of the race" sets in, and within a surprisingly few generations you get pointers that don't point, flushers that don't flush, and retrievers that don't fetch.

So, how *do* you find the right litter? One way, if you've seen a dog you admire (you can broaden your horizons in this respect by attending field trials, hunt tests, and "training days" organized by local dog clubs), is to approach its owner and express an interest in getting a puppy out of it. If the dog you like is a female, you might even offer to pay the stud fee (subject to your approval of the sire) in exchange for the first pick. Along these same lines, another smart move is simply to ask the owners of good dogs where they got them, and if they can direct you to the source.

If you don't have a sire, dam, or bloodline in mind, you need to go into full-blown intelligence-gathering mode, keeping your eyes and ears open and talking to anyone and everyone in a position to provide useful information: fellow sportsmen whose opinions you value, professional trainers, veterinarians, shooting preserve proprietors, field trialers, the list goes on. Follow up on the leads that sound promising by contacting the breeders, some of whom may have literature or websites (although, if at all possible, you should visit their kennels personally and watch their dogs work). Describe what you're looking for, and listen carefully and critically to what they have to say. Remember that if it sounds too good to be true, it probably is.

Before you make any kind of financial commitment—some sort of deposit is the norm—you need to pin down the terms of the health guarantee. This is an absolute must—a "deal breaker," if you will. The standard guarantee for a pup that's diagnosed with a congenital or inherited defect (hip dysplasia being the most common) is a replacement puppy of equal value; some breeders offer a choice of a puppy or a refund of the purchase price.

Speaking of price, well-bred puppies don't come cheap—and pups from long-established kennels or elite breedings can be downright expensive (assuming you consider the low four figures expensive). The thing to remember is that the purchase price is only a fraction of the total financial investment you'll make over the course of your dog's life. Another thing to remember is that it costs as much to feed a pot licker as it does to feed the other kind, the kind dreams—and lasting memories—are made of.

VETTING A DOG TRAINER

There are certain people every sportsman should have in his corner. At the top of this list, for reasons that should be obvious, is an understanding spouse—or at least a forgiving one. A good gunsmith is pretty darn important, too. An attorney and an accountant are the other "musts," assuming all of the aforementioned are a) competent, b) discreet, and c) not currently under investigation.

Depending on your tastes and the way your lifestyle is inclined, you can add to this list *ad infinitum*: butcher, wine merchant, travel agent, bookseller, mechanic, and so on. But for the sportsman who hunts with dogs, any dream team necessarily includes two individuals whose membership is absolutely mandatory. One is a skilled and compassionate veterinarian. The other, of course, is a top-notch professional trainer.

I know a fair number of serious upland bird and waterfowl hunters—people from all walks of life and all parts of the country—who own all breeds of gundogs, and I can count on one hand those who've never used the services of a pro. By definition, serious hunters expect a lot from their dogs, and there are situations and circumstances when a pro is simply better equipped to help a dog reach its full potential. It's not that dog training is rocket science—it isn't—but it does take time, patience, insight (some pros have an uncanny ability to "read" dogs and analyze their behavior), dedication, and the physical resources (grounds, ponds, birds, and so on) to get the job done right.

If you're like most of us, you're probably lacking in one or more of these departments. And if you're honest about your shortcomings—and those of your dog—chances are that at some point you'll want to seek out a professional trainer. The disparity between what you can accomplish and what a pro can accomplish becomes especially obvious when you move beyond the basics and start pushing the envelope with advanced training refinements; when progress stalls and your dog can't seem to get over the hump to the next level; or when your dog develops an intractable problem such as blinking (purposely avoiding birds), bolting (running off and self-hunting), or, worst of all, gun-shyness.

Because we're on the subject, gun-shyness is perhaps the best example of a problem that a professional trainer has the tools and expertise to fix—and that you almost certainly don't. Not that there's any excuse for putting a dog in the position to *become* gun-shy, but you don't want me to get started on that.

Back to the matter at hand, one of the most important things to keep in mind regarding professional training is that when you decide to take your dog to a pro, you need to have a very clear idea of what you want the pro to accomplish. And whether it's curing a specific problem, exposing your dog to a new situation, or taking an essentially untrained dog and developing it into a serviceable gunning companion, you need to communicate your objectives very clearly. Dog training isn't cheap—you should plan on spending $400 to $700 per month for at least two months—and if you and the trainer aren't on the same page, you might as well run your money though a paper shredder.

On the other hand, if you and the pro are able to maintain a close working relationship—and a big part of picking a pro is finding one you feel comfortable with—it can be one of the best investments you ever make.

The cardinal rule of choosing a professional trainer is this: Choose a pro with a proven track record of producing the kind of dog best suited to what, where, and how you hunt. It seems painfully obvious, I know, but a lot of guys, particularly those in the pointing dog camp, ignore it. They get all starry-eyed reading about the exploits of the pros who compete on the major field-trial circuit, and they start thinking that it would be incredibly cool to have one of these hotshots train their dog.

Don't get me wrong, the pros who compete successfully on the major circuit are fabulous trainers. They *have* to be. But there are two things you need to understand. One is that, with rare exceptions, field-trial dogs and gundogs are two very different animals. Many field-trial dogs aren't used for hunting, and even if they were, they wouldn't be very pleasant gunning companions. They're simply too high-powered—"too much dog."

The other thing you should be aware of is that the high-profile pros who even *accept* gundogs—some don't—typically delegate the training to assistants. The role of the boss is, at best, supervisory. Not that the assistant isn't in all likelihood a fine trainer in his own right, but . . .

The point I'm trying to make is that if your objective is a creditable gundog, you're better served patronizing a pro who's primarily, or even exclusively, a gundog trainer. If you can find one in reasonably close proximity to where you live, so much the better. To a man, every pro I've ever talked to has emphasized the importance of "training the owner" at the same time he's training the dog. This is particularly critical with owners who lack hands-on, "in the field" experience with gundogs, although the plain fact is that most of us aren't as expert as we imagine ourselves to be.

"People always tell me they'd like to train their dog themselves, but they just don't have time," said Vincent Guglielmo, who trains pointing dogs for grouse and woodcock hunting at his Chenango Valley Kennels in Greene, New York. "Well, that may be true, but a lot of people really aren't that knowledgeable. They may have read a book or watched a video on training, but there isn't a single method that works with every dog. That's why most pros have a whole 'bag of tricks' they can draw from. We try one thing, and if that doesn't work, we try another, and if that doesn't work, we try another."

Communicating your desires to the pro and spending time with him as he trains your dog is one thing; constantly questioning, second-guessing, and looking over his shoulder, however, is quite another. Like any other professional, a trainer needs the freedom to do it "his way," and if you don't have enough confidence in his program and respect for his abilities to stand back and let him do his job, you'd better find someone who *does* inspire such confidence and respect— or train your dog yourself. Professional trainers tend to be very patient people— it's part of the job description, after all—but more than a few have told clients very explicitly where to go and/or where to put things when said clients have gotten in their faces one too many times. Having observed that everyone who's ever gone hunting with a dog seems to think he's an expert on the subject, I can't say I blame them. The moral is, if you think you know more about training than the trainer does, it's bound to be an unhappy and probably short-lived relationship.

In this same vein, you also need to be objective about your dog's capabilities and limitations. The overwhelming majority of pups from reputable, thoughtful breeders have what it takes, genetically, to make fine gundogs—but not every puppy comes from a reputable, thoughtful breeder. A few years ago I was tagging along with my friend Bob Olson, who trains all breeds of gundogs at his River Road Kennel in Lena, Wisconsin. Bob was working a young pointing dog—the breed doesn't matter—and within a few minutes it was obvious that the pup just didn't have much talent.

Knowing Bob, I knew he wouldn't take a dog for training that was destined to be a washout. In fact, I'd seen him tell potential clients, after evaluating their dogs, that he'd do what he could but that ultimately they'd be throwing good money after bad. So I asked Bob why he hadn't suggested that the client start over with a better prospect. He shrugged and said, "He doesn't need a better dog. He's an older gentleman who does all his hunting on a preserve, and it's really less important that the dog help him than that it doesn't *hurt* him. He just likes the idea of hunting with a dog, and as long as it doesn't give him any trouble and points the occasional bird, he'll be happy."

Good pros can accomplish amazing things, but they're not magicians; the quality of the final product still depends, to a great extent, on what they have to work with. As Bob likes to say, "My favorite dogs to train are the ones that make *me* look good." This is why many trainers insist on an approval period (usually about two weeks or so) before they formally accept new prospects. Third-generation pro Dave Lorenz of The Hogan Kennels in Ingleside, Illinois, bluntly explains the rationale: "I'm not about to waste my time—and the owner's money—on a dog that isn't going to cut it."

So how do you find the trainer that's right for you, your dog, and your style of hunting? Very simple: You solicit recommendations from people who are in a position to know. In other words, you "network." You ask your friends, you talk to the proprietors of shooting preserves and hunt clubs (many of which have a "resident" pro or a close relationship with one), and you seek out experienced sportsmen and pay attention to what they have to say. As in just about every other realm you can think of, the more information you have, the better your chances of making a sound decision.

For example, a few months ago a friend in Montana e-mailed that his brother in upstate New York was looking for a trainer for his young golden retriever. Knowing I had some contacts in that area, my friend wondered if I could give him a name. "Let me make some calls," I said, "and I'll get back to you."

I made a couple of calls to people whose opinions I trust, and the same name came up both times: Ted McCue, who trains out of the Verbank Gun Club, in Verbank, New York. I relate this not to give a gratuitous plug to Mr. McCue, whom I've never met (or even spoken to), but because I think it's pretty typical of the way these deals play out. It's a matter of degrees of separation: The first guy you talk to may not have an answer, but he can probably put you onto someone who does—or at least get you pointed in the right direction.

As Tom Ness, who stays busy training spaniels and retrievers at his Oahe Kennels in Menoken, North Dakota, puts in, "My business is based on two things: word-of-mouth and the people who've seen my dogs at cocker field trials. There's no difference between cocker field-trial dogs and cocker gundogs; the dogs I run in trials are the dogs I hunt with. Hopefully—unlike what's happened with other breeds—it'll stay that way."

Of course, a professionally trained dog you've seen or hunted over that has impressed you is undoubtedly the best recommendation of all. After that it becomes a matter of vetting the pro to make sure he's someone you feel comfortable with, that his kennels are scrupulously clean and secure (if not necessarily fancy), and that he has the facilities and personnel to do the job. Indeed, one of the hallmarks of a "pro's pro" is his willingness to answer questions, show you around, and invite you to observe him at work.

There are never any guarantees when it comes to dogs, but there are ways to narrow the odds.

GETTING THE MOST OUT OF AN OLDER DOG

Gallantry is a word you don't hear much any more. But in thinking about the way that older dogs shrug off the insults of age and soldier on, their desire undiminished and their great heart on display for all the world to see, it seems just right. Old dogs perform with gallantry.

And while there'll be a little stiffness in their gait, while they may not carry their tails so high, and while you'll probably have to lift them over fences they used to leap, they still bring plenty to the party. Experience, wisdom, even guile: These are the compensations for the erosion of physical skills, and they're irreplaceable. As Muddy Waters put it in one of his lyrics, "A young horse is fast, but an old horse knows what's goin' on."

Getting the most out of your gray-muzzled veteran requires that you recognize its limitations, manage it intelligently in the field, and be vigilant about maintaining its health and keeping it in the best physical condition possible. Dogs age at different rates, the rule of thumb being that the bigger the dog, the sooner it begins to show the effects of aging. Generally speaking, though, by the time your pal is eight to nine years old, you'll want to start treating it as a "senior." The same things that have always been important—proper diet, lots of exercise, regular visits to the vet—still are; they're just *more* so.

Many veterinarians recommend that older dogs be given an annual blood chemistry panel, including tests for kidney and liver function, so that potential problems can be detected and treated before they become serious. The blood work will also reveal any diet- or nutrition-related concerns that need to be addressed. A chest film and electrocardiogram are good ideas, too, both in terms of identifying problems and establishing a "baseline" for future reference.

Another thing many vets suggest is that you bring older dogs in more frequently for checkups—twice-a-year, for example, instead of the usual once—so that they can better monitor their overall health and note any changes that may occur. Trips to the vet aren't free, of course, and not every sportsman is in a position to bankroll the ideal veterinary agenda. (I know I'm not.) Be upfront with your vet about what you can (and can't) afford, so that the two of you can tailor a program that gives your dog the most bang for your buck.

Undoubtedly the most common ailment in older dogs—especially dogs who subject their joints to significant wear and tear in the field—is arthritis. The good news is that veterinary science has made great strides in this area, primarily through prescription anti-inflammatory drugs like Rimadyl. It's no exaggeration to say that these medications have extended the careers of literally thousands of hunting dogs. Dr. Marty Smith of Doctors Foster & Smith in Rhinelander, Wisconsin, told me about a springer spaniel so crippled by arthritis that its owner was about to have it euthanized. Within a few days of being put on Rimadyl, it was racing around like a pup again.

Over-the-counter treatments for joint care have their place as well, notably glucosamine and chondroitin sulfate. These "nutraceuticals," long available as dietary supplements in tablet or powder form, are increasingly finding their way into commercial dog foods. However your hunting partner gets them, they help repair damaged cartilage and promote the production of synovial fluid, the "lubricant" found in healthy joints. Many sportsmen whose dogs' symptoms aren't severe enough to warrant Rimadyl achieve excellent results using glucosamine and chondroitin sulfate in combination with simple buffered aspirin.

Maintaining muscle tone with regular exercise also promotes healthy joints (loss of tone can lead to painful "bone-on-bone" situations), as does keeping your dog in fighting trim. Excess weight stresses the joints; plus, obesity in dogs presents the same litany of risks it does in people: heart disease, diabetes, liver and digestive disorders, and so forth. Exercise, again, plays an important role, but it has to share the stage with diet. Most older dogs will benefit from a "senior" diet higher in fiber and lower in fat and protein, although for a few weeks before and then during the hunting season, you should switch to a diet with more fat—the best source of fuel for hard-working gundogs of *any* age.

A somewhat overlooked aspect of the senior-care equation is kenneling. Older dogs are simply less tolerant of temperature extremes, and while it's important to provide adequate shade in the summertime, I think it's even more critical, in particular with short-coated breeds like pointers, vizslas, and GSPs, to keep them warm in the winter. I've seen several cases in which I'm convinced ramshackle kenneling in bitterly cold conditions led to premature aging.

It comes back to recognizing the older dog's limitations—which, in turn, brings us to management in the field. I'd say it's a matter of using common sense, but common sense doesn't seem to be very common any more.

What you have to remember is that while the skills and stamina wane, the desire to hunt burns as bright and hot as ever. If you let it, it'll drive your beloved companion beyond his physical limits. You need to treat your older dog like an elite athlete in the twilight of his career, husbanding his strength—which includes making sure he never lacks for food, water, and a place either to cool down or warm up—and carefully picking his spots. If you're going to err, err on the side of caution and leave him in the truck.

He won't be very happy about that, but if it means one more day—hell, one more *hour*—of hunting together . . . well, I don't know anybody who calls himself a dog person who wouldn't take that trade.

Index

A

American water spaniels, 119, 120

Arthritis, 148

B

Bird hunting, 66–69, 70, 82–85, 87–137
  breeds for, 112–14
  choosing puppy for, 140–42
  for grouse & woodcock, 98–100, 102, 116, 118
  for pheasants, 119–24, 133, 136–37
  pickup dogs, 126–32, 136
  for quail, 94, 101–2, 105–6, 108, 110–12
  for waterfowl, 90, 104–5

Boykin spaniels, 106–7, 112

Breeds. *See* specific breeds

Brittanys, 10–11, 124, 133
  bird hunting with, 87–89, 94, 101–2, 108

Buckingham, Nash, 103

C

Catlin, George, 29

Chesapeake Bay retrievers, **32,** 94–95, 119, 136, 137
  for bird hunting, 105, 118

Clumber spaniels, 134

Cocker spaniels. *See* English cocker spaniels

Continental breeds. *See also* specific breeds, 124, 133

Crangle, Earl, 34–35, 40

D

de Boilieu, Lambert, 71

de la Valdéne, Guy, 108

DeLoia, Joe, 104

Diet
  and living indoors, 19
  for older dogs, 149

Dogs. *See* Sporting breeds; specific breeds

Dohse, Ray, 44

Dove hunting. *See also* Bird hunting, 91

E

Encyclopedia of North American Sporting Dogs, The, 140

English cocker spaniels, 112, 114–15, 134, 136, 140

English setters, 26, 116–17, 119, 140
  and grouse hunting, 98–100
  Hillbright Susanna, 34–35, 40
  Johnny Crockett, 42
  pictures of, **20, 38, 59, 66, 67, 83, 84, 92, 97**